I0749527

# Sightings Along the Journey

# Sightings Along the Journey

Carroll Blair

Aveon Publishing Company

ISBN: 978-1-936430-43-7

Library of Congress Control Number
2011903966

Aveon Publishing Co.
P.O. Box 380739
Cambridge, MA 02238-0739 USA

Also by Carroll Blair

*Grains of Thought*
*Facing the Circle*
*Reel to Real*
*Shifting Tides*
*Reaches*
*Out of Silence*
*Quarter Notes*
*By Rays of Light*
*Into the Inner Life*
*Gnosis of the Heart*
*Soul Reflections*
*Beneath and Beyond the Surface*
*Of Courage and Commitment*
*For Today and Tomorrow*
*In Meditation*
*Through Desert's Fire*
*Offerings to Pilgrims*
*Human Natures*
*(Of Animal and Spiritual)*
*Atoms from the Suns of Solitude*
*Colors of Devotion*
*Voicings*
*Through the Shadows*
*As the World Winds Flow*

Wherever one is, or
one goes, Life is ever
whispering . . . Behold.

Since the beginning of thought the search has been for what is beyond thought, yet is before one (and within one).

What is always is always here and everywhere, but is the same as being nowhere to the life that has not ventured to perceive through the spiritual.

The spiritual journey is not to a place, but to an awareness of spiritual presence — (then on to ever-growing awareness . . . )

Until it is journeyed the way cannot be known.

Many steps forward on the path
are through the maze of ego-ignorance,
moving beyond the maze when enough
steps have been taken.

Going further into light more truth
is revealed; going further into truth
more light is revealed.

To embrace the journey is to
discover what the journey is for.

The power to transform, to grow
given to human-being is among the most
beautiful and mysterious of
human phenomena.

Each human life is a wilderness of
virgin forest filled with wonder and
challenge, meant to be lived
like no other.

As it is used, the spiritual power
of a life becomes more.

Confinement to the rational can take one only so far, like a ferry crossing a body of water to transport one to another shore.

The world enters through the senses, bringing infinitely more than those of a day-to-day sentience are able to detect.

It is the inner eye [the spiritual eye] that must be open before one can truly see.

The amount of light and truth one is able to see is the amount that one has prepared oneself to perceive.

One's path awaits one's steps.

As a dancer feels a oneness with where she has stepped, so there is a sense of oneness with the paths of spiritual aspirants, reassuring them that where they are is just where they need to be.

The path is where all spiritual seed of a life is planted, blossoming as if by magic, further along the path.

With every awakening new life
is entering into being.

Like the universe, the spirit of
gathering light is ever expanding.

A spiritual journey is a universe unto
itself, experiences coalescing, collecting
into mass like atoms to form galaxies of
thought and emotion, creating orders
of beauty and complexity held together
by a gravity of soul.

The way of enlightenment is one
of destinations, but no Destination.

It is the energy of the eternal that
holds the extraordinary of life.

To live as if passing through the world only once, but living through the spiritual of one's being is to experience the essence of eternity — as if living for all time — (and beyond time).

Reality is of the profound and everlasting; all else is but the dream of the fleeting.

Upon everything true and beautiful lies the imprint of the divine.

Where there is grace
strength must also be.

Much is missed when failing to notice the many subtle blessings on the way to higher blessing.

It is the valley that accents the wonder of the peak.

As with physics, the study of life has for the aspirant its micro view and its macro view.

What is properly appreciated is properly understood regarding the measure of its value.

A powerful insight is worth more than a thousand impressions from the shallows.

Thought alone cannot bring one to profound understanding. True enlightenment is that of the mind, the heart, the spirit harmonizing as one.

A journey is like study — of benefit only when attention is being paid.

Life is always here, is always now,
beckoning to be discovered, inviting
all to join to the power of its truth.

The natural world beams with
creativeness, mirroring the possibilities,
the birthright that lives in the soul
of human-being.

The creative spirit and growing spirit
are one, exploring layer after layer,
depth after depth of the spiritual quest.

Life isn't something that just happens
to have dance, poetry, music . . . it is
(at its best), dance, poetry, and music
shining through eternal light.

They impede their growth of vision
who do not take with them throughout their lives the natural wonder
of the child.

The spiritual journey is in essence the journey from life [one's life] to Life, through Life.

The journey is a discovery of not only what is, but also what is not.

Rife is the temporal with misperceptions
of regression taken for progression.

To partake and rejoice in all
that matters is to turn away
from what doesn't matter.

The spirit of light is homeless,
is placeless, as it should be, as it
needs to be to stay the path of light.

Of greater importance than the
pace is the direction of the journey.

The spiritual must be engaged
stripped of all I's and me's before
a realization of its gifts
may be achieved.

Ego opens doors to the lives it rules
that are best left closed and keeps
closed others that would be of great
benefit to have open.

To give up allegiance to the material world is not to lose, but to gain a truer world.

As a particle of dust passing before an endless dawn is the material to the spiritual.

It is the endeavor that is powered
by the infinite that lifts one
beyond one's self and brings
one to higher Self
[to the higher Oneness].

Animal energy is not a testament to
being *alive* in the human sense . . .
[in the spiritual sense].

True power begins to breathe,
to come alive in one's life when
it is realized that the origin of
its source is not oneself, but
something far greater, which
one is just a part of.

Attachment to ego
is the barrier to union
of a profound nature.

Ego is like the wizard behind the curtain of fanciful OZ: full of roar and promises, but all of empty smoke.

The illusions of the day-to-day change, but its Illusion of Reality remains.

They live in shadow despite any spotlight from the temporal who grasp at the shadows of life.

Going with the flow of the day-to-day leads to nowhere. Going with the flow of the spiritual leads to bliss . . . (and more than bliss).

In the temporal there are countless
desires for the trivial pursued by the
misguidance of fear and ignorance;
in the spiritual there is only one:
the realization of the divine.

Before it can be lived the beginnings
of a spiritual life must first be achieved.

Every advance of an earthly character
that one makes is another compromise,
creating further distance between oneself
and the eternal of one's life.

The everyday world is a show of games
that all must choose for themselves
which ones (if any) are worth
their while to play.

A bird's domain is the sky, but if
held to the ground from being snared
by a trap, the sky is no longer hers
to spread her wings upon and be
what she was meant to be.

The difference between the appearance
of truth, and truth, is like the difference
between running water from a kitchen
faucet and that from a mountain brook.

To cling to the fleeting is like trying to hold on to a raft for dear life, but the raft is sinking, and also fading taking the best from their lives who refuse to let go.

Dedication to the temporal can only stifle inner growth and close the way to spiritualization.

They have not looked deeply inside or out who haven't recognized the indelible truth that the way to substantive growth has nothing to do with ego.

Ego's vision of the world projects no further in relation to all that may be envisioned than the weight one may lift or carry in relation to the immeasurable weight of the physical universe.

Before reading the eye of Existence
one must be free from the "I"
of one's existence.

No more than the precise temperature
of a climate can be assessed by how warm
or cold a body feels can life's truths
be assessed by means of the
subjective or personal.

The world is full of misunderstandings,
none of them coming from the world.

The true nature of things hides
from no eyes — it is eyes [and more
than eyes] that often hide from
the truth of their nature.

Many conflicts of the world are not a
condition of truth clashing with truth,
but illusion clashing with illusion.

The sun shines from above lighting the
earth, but time and again does humankind
reveal itself to be living in darkness.

More challenging is the spiritual advancement than the technological, and meaningless is the latter as well as dangerous without the progress and guidance of the former.

It is through the spiritual that a capacity for reverence is attained that moves one to honor what is worthy of being honored.

What keeps humankind from the experience of paradise is not a banishment caused by original sin but its general disregard for the immortal, choosing to live mainly for the pursuit of the unimportant instead of having always at the forefront of its vision the duty to serve and cherish what is of principal importance — which is and of the immortal.

Before humankind can come to order it must first come to Life.

Spiritual evolution is not something that happens externally, but inside oneself — individual by individual, one by one.

Central to human growth and
development is a grappling with
what it means to be human.

Humankind is unaware of all that it is capable, and equally unaware of the cost of its realization.

It is often said that humanity will one day be better than it is today, but it will only be what it is now and has been (or worse) if the work that is necessary to make changes for the better remains undone. (And such work could never be finished, for each generation would need to renew the commitment and all that it necessitates to live through the finer nature of human-being.)

If the evils of the world are ever to be defeated, the spiritual dimension must be widely served.

Nothing does the world more harm than selfishness. Nothing does the world more good than action rooted in selflessness.

The life of true power is one
that is free of the desire for power.

One nation at war with another,
one people at war with another,
but in truth it is man at war
with himself.

Consider all the space ego
takes up in human life, and
how that space could be filled
with love, beauty and wisdom
if it were gone.

Examine many a “need” closely
and one will find only an ego-want.

Among the first impulses to bestir one
to a higher state of being is the
shifting from a primary interest
in a standard of living to the
standard of one’s life.

No more can the spiritual be nourished
by material possession than the body can be
nourished by the consumption of sand.

The false coin of the world depletes when it is spent. The true augments.

It is not possible to live large or grand without a grandness of heart and spirit.

There is animal will, and spiritual will.

When one turns his attention away from needless wants of the personal to the legitimate needs of others, it is turning toward the spiritual with the eye of the spiritual.

One can see more when there
is less of oneself in the picture.

Ego is either outgrown, or remains
a lifelong hindrance to growth.

A blessing taken for granted could
never give to a life the benefit
that could be given.

There is always another truth,
another beauty to create or discover.

In spiritual evolution there are no preconceptions brought to a moment about the moment — only an openness to engage the fullness of its presence.

Life simply is, but is far from simple
in the depths of its wonders.

To keep in mind that there is more
than what has been seen and experienced
is to remain open to possible instruction
from all that is encountered.

There is no end to what Life has
to teach — only an end to a
willingness to learn.

It is in wonder that the highest alertness is attained.

To give up the ego is like trading a pebble stone for the treasures of the sea.

Growth demands that the fear for security be abandoned, for it is to be born to something new, to something more, and what is newborn must be vulnerable for a time to its surroundings, including those of the spiritual.

There are as many potential
births in the spiritual of a life
as there are will and courage
enough to bring them forth,
each bearing gifts greater
than the one before.

There is a difference between relieving hunger and satisfying it. Regarding the metaphysical it is better if the hunger is never satisfied, for it leads one to strive further for deeper wisdom and light.

The spirit also has its deserts that
must be crossed to earn its gifts,
to know its love.

Truth is the great calm, but
it is also the great storm.

The face of enlightenment is the
face of serenity, but ordeals must
be experienced before it is attained.

It is the quake from within that
frees the fruit of the soul.

The crux of the journey is not a
leisurely saunter, it is a labor.

One goes only so far as one's
courage and strength will allow,
but each day brings new opportunity
to create more of what is needed
to carry on.

Growth cannot be realized in the life that seeks to stay in the comfort zone.

The journey is not always of grace, though each step forward is one of grace.

As it is not possible to go from age twenty to age thirty overnight, so one cannot go from being undisciplined and uncommitted to developing all that is required to reach an advanced stage of enlightenment in a short period of time.

Nowhere is the characteristic of wanting something for nothing more widely demonstrated throughout humankind than in the matter of spirituality — wanting enlightenment without working for it, salvation without suffering for it.

The enlightened soul knows that life's pains are essential to growth, and thus, a gift.

It is in the throes of spiritual struggle
that a reality of freedom is born.

What is difficult is perceived and
accepted by the discerning aspirant
as beneficial.

For certain things to be cleansed
they must be wiped, scrubbed,
not handled with kid gloves . . .
wise would it be to expect the
cleansing of a life to be the same.

The great triumph in life is the
surrender to Life. (But this is not
to surrender the responsibility for
one's growth and development.)

No cause is there for rejoice when
what one has spent a lifetime building
is terminated — unless it is ego.

Among the great gifts of life is the epiphany that there is a better way, a more noble way to live that is not directed by ego, not driven by selfish desires and cravings for worldly power and position — that only love, truth, wisdom and beauty are worth treasuring and living for, guided by a selflessness of heart, mind and spirit.

To live through the spiritual of human-being is to be in light; to live through the animal is to be in darkness.

Far from the light of the divine is the closed mind and heart.

It is through humility that all that is good enters and goes forth from human life.

There is a distinction between serving to live and living to serve.

A true rebel for the cause of
humanity is one who accepts the
challenges and demands of the
solitary odyssey to the transcendent.

The noble of spirit seek not
a place of honor, but a path
that is honorable.

To be progressively giving
more to life than taking
from life is to be going
the way of the spiritual.

The sincere life is not one
without error, but one whose
direction is true.

Nothing is lost by leaving
the temporal behind.

With every ego-want eliminated
one's inner wealth is increased.

When blessing is received it is not for one to hold on to, but to share and contribute in some manner to the lives of others.

The wise of all ages see the truth of all ages.

Endeavor without the spiritual behind it is empty and void of meaning.

A life's energy weakens when used for the bidding of the shallow; strengthens when used in the service of the everlasting.

Passing through life are all, but it is what one is drawn to and connects with that moves one to do or not do more, to be or not be more than of the passing.

All good things are as instruments filled with music waiting for the soul to play them.

Love is the purest manifest of the divine.

Love, wisdom, truth . . . they too have their impostors in operation throughout the world.

Nowhere in the worldly is anything generated that comes close to the power and depth of what emanates from the eternal.

Revolution means nothing if it is not followed by spiritual evolution.

Though water is a destroyer of fire,
a cup of it is not enough to
quell a raging blaze — the same
with good and evil.

When humankind looks to make life
less challenging it becomes more
menacing for all.

The more one loves the greater one's responsibility to life, but the more it is welcome.

To produce, like harvests of the seasons, to give away . . . to produce again, to (again) give what is harvested away . . . this, the life of the spirit moved by love and magnanimity.

Windows of opportunity are open not only to go in and take, but also to give.

With love nothing is taken for granted.

The enlightened spirit doesn't consider an innate talent or gift to be a possession, but a fortuity for which the recipient is blessed by its presence.

Little time have they to lament a misfortune in their lives who are grateful for their blessings.

The noble quality has about it the look of the ageless.

To see beyond negatives is not to forget that they exist.

Sometimes it is not a matter of building on what has gone before, but avoiding a chasm that's been left behind.

An error by an individual may take minutes to correct; centuries can elapse before an error by humankind is resolved.

One may not always hear
through the noise and
commotions of the world,
but one may learn to
see through them.

The more spiritually evolved
the more cause one can see
behind an effect.

It is when the fight for something good
and noble has been won and the air begins
to settle that evil makes its way back into the
fold, infiltrating with stealth and cunning
the ground that it has lost, regaining
its strength and staking its position
to fight another day.

Poison is not poison to itself; evil, not evil.

For justice to prevail over an injustice of the world is difficult, but even more challenging is holding ground after the battle has been won.

Betrayal shows everywhere around the compromise of integrity.

The eyes that are always looking down
or looking up never see clearly
what is before them.

Sight as well as sound can be
disturbing to a peace.

The day-to-day seems without limits
in its accommodations of the false,
but Life can only use [will only accept]
what is true.

As a cloud is the day-to-day
hiding the sun of the eternal.

A little spiritual instinct outweighs
a store of school-bound information
in navigating one's way
through the world.

Not in the earthly will the
eternal on earth be found.

Like prey moving toward the spider's web, lives are lived by many unaware of the consequences of their direction, going along without forethought, impelled by animal-will, comprehending too late where they have placed themselves, to be devoured in ways they could never have dreamed.

Within the price for entry into higher states of awareness is a giving up of more from the temporal.

Because a life is busy doesn't
necessarily mean that it is full.

To do well in the worldly sense can
time and again be accomplished
without being well in the spiritual.

It is the most maculate objects that exhibit the clearest picture of where they have been.

True principles are born in a profound privacy of the soul and protected by that privacy, not to be compromised by outer force.

The greatest things are of those which the interests of the everyday world have no use for.

The way to inner peace requires
a warlike courage.

One needs time to discover the
higher truth, but it will not be found
in the field of time.

Ever lost is human life without
reverence for the spiritual.

The more humble the spirit the more powerful it grows.

Who knows not gratitude knows not love nor wisdom nor bliss.

The enlightened begin by doing the work of the mind, then proceed to that of the heart and spirit.

A book in hand means nothing if its content is not transmitted to consciousness. Likewise, experience amounts to nothing if what it has to teach is not taken to mind and heart.

Only the humble can teach
the highest things, because
only the humble can learn them.

Around or in or of
the profound, ego is
not to be found.

To reduce ignorance is to increase knowledge; to reduce stupidity is to increase wisdom.

A gentleness of heart is not achieved by going easy on oneself or being gentle with one's faults.

Without courage the best of human life and of humankind cannot be realized.

The way to light is far from a freedom from the dark.

The means to the treasure is
part of the treasure.

Life is earned by giving it away.

In service one finds [one
creates] purpose.

To turn away from the worldly
is to turn in the direction
of eternal grace.

For the saint, the artist, the sage,
a day of rest is a day of preparation
for future days of work.

With love there is no end; without
love there is no beginning.

As long as the journey goes on
the discovery goes on.

The Great Blessing of Life is that
it is filled with countless blessings.

To peer into the soul of Life is to
peer into the soul of Truth.

When living through the eternal of one's being it matters not where one's body is in space and time or in what place in the material universe, for the eternal is untouched by all causation of the temporal, unaffected by manifest of the fleeting, holding the divine power of what is true and everlasting.

What moves the mind to bliss,
the spirit to soar, the heart to
sing . . . this, the Great Reality.

## ABOUT THE AUTHOR

Carroll Blair is an author of more than twenty books and the recipient of numerous awards. His work has been well endorsed and commendably reviewed. Among his titles cited for distinction are *Through the Shadows*, winner of the Pacific Book Awards, and *Quarter Notes*, winner of the Sharp Writ Book Awards. He is an alumnus of the Boston Conservatory and lives in Massachusetts.

www.ingramcontent.com/pod-product-compliance
Lightning Source LLC
LaVergne TN
LVHW050934080826
845145LV00004B/1263